# NORTH BANK NIGHT

*by*

EDWARD STOREY

CHATTO AND WINDUS

THE HOGARTH PRESS

1969

Published by
Chatto and Windus Ltd
with The Hogarth Press Ltd
42 William IV Street
London WC2

★

Clarke, Irwin and Co Ltd
Toronto

SBN 7011 1459 2

Printed in Great Britain by
T. H. Brickell and Son Ltd
The Blackmore Press, Gillingham, Dorset

*The Phoenix Living Poets*

NORTH BANK NIGHT

*The Phoenix Living Poets*

★

ALEXANDER BAIRD: *Poems*

ALAN BOLD: *To Find the New*

GEORGE MACKAY BROWN: *The Year of the Whale*

GLORIA EVANS DAVIES: *Words – for Blodwen*

PATRIC DICKINSON: *This Cold Universe*
*The World I see*

D. J. ENRIGHT: *Addictions · The Old Adam*
*Some Men are Brothers · Unlawful Assembly*

JOHN FULLER: *Fairground Music*
*The Tree that Walked*

DAVID GILL: *Men Without Evenings*

J. C. HALL: *The Burning Hare*

MOLLY HOLDEN: *To Make Me Grieve*

JOHN HORDER: *A Sense of Being*

P. J. KAVANAGH: *On the Way to the Depot*

RICHARD KELL: *Control Tower*

LAURIE LEE: *The Sun my Monument*

LAURENCE LERNER: *The Directions of Memory*

EDWARD LOWBURY: *Time for Sale*
*Daylight Astronomy*

NORMAN MACCAIG: *Measures · A Round of Applause*
*A Common Grace · Surroundings · Rings on a Tree*

JAMES MERRILL: *Nights and Days · Selected Poems*

RUTH MILLER: *Selected Poems*

LESLIE NORRIS: *Finding Gold*

ROBERT PACK: *Selected Poems*

ADRIENNE RICH: *Selected Poems*

JON SILKIN: *Nature with Man*
*The Re-ordering of the Stones*

JON STALLWORTHY: *Root and Branch*

GILLIAN STONEHAM: *When that April*

TERENCE TILLER: *Notes for a Myth*

SYDNEY TREMAYNE: *The Swans of Berwick*

LOTTE ZURNDORFER: *Poems*

# Contents

Acknowledgements are made to the following magazines in which some of these poems have appeared *The Countryman, The Critical Quarterly, Enigma, The Listener, The Poetry Review, The Review of English Literature, P.E.N. New Poems 1965/6, The Poetry Makers* and *B.B.C. Midland Poets.*

*"I remember a house where all were good*
*To me, God knows, deserving no such thing..."*

GERARD MANLEY HOPKINS

## Kingdom of Mist

I ride through a kingdom of mist
where farms drown in a phantom sea
and May piles up in the hedge like snow
waiting to melt in tomorrow's sun.

Young wheat lies down where May-winds blew
and larks are earthbound by the stars.
A heron glides between the trees
that hold the river to its course.

Here pebbles slowly turn to snails
and spiders' webs are spun with glass.
Small shells fly off as frightened moths
and cows become as druid stones.

Only the mist moves as a ghost
loving the land with limbs of fur
and whispered words grow grey as breath
rising into the frosting air.

And night comes down where day once grew,
lights ripple through this thin white sea,
while in the village children sleep
never to know they slept in sky.

## The Visit

I remember her annual coming,
her arms aching with blackberries,
a dead hare hanging from her wrist.
To me she came from a land where grass
lapped like the sea at her house,
where long and soft-eared animals
were carelessly caught, and trees
grew ancient with apples. Nothing changed.
Yearly she came with her thin voice
and dried-apricot face to be kissed.

Now, more than thirty years past,
I see my own mother enter our house,
her arms filled with a new summer
of plums and blackcurrants, her cheeks
lined with the part that now she plays.
Watching her thoughtful and tired eyes
gauging the impact of our joy
I feel surprised that we have shared
this casual acceptance of events—
the young and old at once familiar.

## In Memory of My Grandfather

Swearing about the weather he walked in
like an old tree and sat down;
his beard charred with tobacco, his voice
rough as the bark of his cracked hands.

Whenever he came it was the wrong time.
Roots spread over the hearth, tripped
whoever tried to move about the room—
the house was cramped with only furniture.

But I was glad of his coming. Only
through him could I breathe in the sun
and the smell of fields. His clothes reeked
of the soil and the world outside;

Geese and cows were the colour he made them,
he knew the language of birds and brought them
singing out of his beard, alive
to my blankets. He was winter and harvest.

Plums shone in his eyes when he rambled
of orchards. With giant thumbs he'd split
an apple through the core, and juice
flowed from his ripe, uncultured mouth.

Then, hearing the room clock chime,
he walked from my ceiling of farmyards
and returned to his forest of thunder.
The house regained silence and corners.

Slumped there in my summerless season
I longed for his rough hands and words
to break the restrictions of my bed,
to burst like a tree from my four walls.

But there was no chance again of miming
his habits or language. Only now,
years later in a cramped city, can I
be grateful for his influence and love.

## Birthnight

You wouldn't remember
thirty years ago, breaking
for the first time into the dim light
of a cramped bedroom.

It was a cold night
with earth suffering a severe winter.
Blinds kept from the prying stars
our room's hunger.

Your birth troubled no-one.
I waited, quiet as the stairs
or poker-work text on the wall
or the new born snow.

I felt joy at your coming.
Even when nerves stretched me to crying
and you seemed forever falling,
even to this world I hurried you.

Then suddenly all fire
let loose, more lights were lit,
and to our narrow lives you came
to wreck with cries our customary sleep.

## Cart-horse Preacher

It would have been no use
using the smooth liturgical words
of a cosy religion.
His congregation left their work
in the wet fields of the fen-country,
their cracked hands swollen
with beet-chopping.

To have asked them into the stiff pews
of a cold church would have meant
shouting at air; he knew
the hollow stillness of that place
left them more frozen than the fields,
and holy whining more than winter
lined their face.

So he gathered them round him
on the market square, saying
"I'll speak a language you can understand,
who cares about the lovely use of words
when half the words are nothing more than sound".
Their frost-blue ears were tingled
by his fire.

They met him every Sunday-night and knew
God would be called a muck-heap
or a cow, and no irreverence meant.
"Crops thrive" he'd say, "where muck is spread,  ·
and milk pumps life in every sucker's mouth".
He solved the mystery of their fields,
healed their backs.

But now he's dead, and God's
locked in His church, stiff and alone.
Men work their days out on the land
wondering why the old cart-horse preacher
bothered them at all. Sometimes they feel
without him frost stays longer in their hands
and limbs more often ache.

## Beet-Hoers

For three days those few women
have hoed that long field of sugar beet,
their blue and red cardigans
reduced to the size
of cornflower or poppy.

They have chopped at the weeds
with a precision older than clockwork.
Their arms have a rhythm
that goes back
almost to Adam.

Remote from our world
(if only momentarily)
they work as a tribe to themselves
under a sky
the colour of larkspur.

Monotonous furrows
stretch into a pattern of hours,
a giant sundial
over whose face they move
like a regular shadow.

## Part of a Journey

For a few moments we stop on a dark road
to watch the bright fires of corn stubble –
an invasion of flames over the night fields.

To the unquestioning eye the harvest is done,
grain-driers are full, the baled straw dry,
and most of the tackle stripped down and cleaned.

All that remained uncleaned was the land,
but now this fire moves in with its crackling guns
to purge old roots from the clinging ground.

Under the fens' exaggerated sky the blaze
excites, making a scene that Nero might have shared
when all his world was bouncing under fire.

Like him we are elated by the sight until
someone explains that under those fierce flames
innocent creatures panic, lose their lives,

and what in this dark moment stirs our blood
will, when calm daylight covers the charred earth,
fill us with guilt, as morning always does.

B

## The Return

Little has changed.
The hot evening could, I believe,
belong to any year. Men,
with their shirt-sleeves rolled,
sit talking still outside their houses
or, tired with a hard day's work,
watch silently the martins' loud attempt
to break the speed record.

I know their terraced homes breed heat.
Their stuffy bedrooms defy sleep.
So many generations here have kept
a truce with summer on their steps.
It is a common ritual that few
are willing to forget. They
pass their habits down
like ornaments.

After the brickfields' burning day
they treasure these last cooling hours,
feeling the comfort on parched backs
of air that has not passed through fires.
They saw their fathers take this time
to let the blistered fingers breathe
or place calm evening
on their eyes.

When I first left this clay-pit town
to learn a different choice of words
I thought ten years would see a change,
but coming back from twice that time
it feels as if I changed my mind
and that same morning
turned around.

## Strange Bird

Clay-grey the scraggy heron haunts
    the narrow waters of the Nene,
half-bird, half-spirit now he stands
    quiet as the grass and waiting stones.

Each night I come to find him here
    where mist has power to disguise
the breadth of river and protect
    me from his cold and glassy eyes.

And if I move or make a sound
    with ghostlike wings he floats away,
a stretch of river-bank in flight,
    a heavy shadow from the sky.

## North Bank Night

Tonight the cold air magnifies the sky,
loose nets of cloud are strung about the stars
and distant lights of cities rim the night
bright as the late owl's frosty claws.

Tonight the sky has space about its ears,
a million years from sun to blazing sun,
and darkness feels as tangible as fire
that burns the face and scars the ungloved hand.

Tonight the grass and hedges sweat with ice,
the river locks the stars behind its glass,
and that lone bird that swooped across the fields
is caught by hungry winter and devoured.

## Experience

He stood as useless
as a dumb scarecrow
while the March gales
reduced the weight
of his fields –
brown clouds of soil
darkening the sky,
changing the shape of furrows
and fen drains.

He had done all
that was possible
to marry his land
to the Spring seed,
but strong winds
had planed the earth dry
and powdered the clods
to a fine dust – less gentle
than May mist.

Neighbours had warned
that the fields would move
and he could see now
why they had questioned
his young hopes –
tattered in spirit,
like an old coat, he dreamt
dejectedly of crops
he would not reap.

## Summer

Removed from winter the sky blossoms.
Trees hatch from their black shells,
fledgelings tremble like leaves trying to fly.

Over the water the fishing-rods of boys
make bars of music. Bream laze
in a minim of sunlight, and the stream

shimmers with cymbals. Hidden from gunsight
a fox sleeps in a boy's arms. Hares
leap through a forest of cornstalks.

Even the roads drowse out their long miles,
making earth shine with the bright beads
of their black sweat.

## Three Fears

That was the first fear of waiting.
The gasmantle fading to a pale star,
the kitchen cupboard filling up with ghosts,
and crickets chanting from a black-lead grate.

Then I was five and full of troubled sleep.
To be alone for even half-an-hour
in that small house was all eternity.
I felt to die would ease my trembling.

Years later in a different room,
where half a lifetime had been drifting by,
I waited for my love to come back home,
to bring back warmth to that cold emptiness.

Then I was young and did not understand
the tolling bell and shadows at the door.
I did not know what grief would plague my mind
or wear endurance to the bone.

Today in a strange, indifferent house
where fires pale beside the meter's tick,
I tremble now beyond the mortal nerve
and fear the longer waiting I must keep.

## Death in Winter

Crouched like a bush brittle with winter
he prepared to spend the night under a tree.

Already the clothes in nearby gardens
hung stiff as cardboard on the lines.

Hunchbacked with the cold his grey beard
spread a blanket on his chest.

His eyes shut out the patches of warm light
from neighbouring houses.

Car headlamps scissored the frozen fields.
Snow came and camouflaged fences.

In the morning he did not feel the sun.
They stretched his body out and took him home.

## South Creake

*for Anthony Scott*

What violence will expose this peace
or shatter flame-light on cool stone.
Will the respect of ritual or myth
survive beyond the shadow of a faith.

This ancient tower stands against the rain
and darkness deepens with its mystery.
What low-blown whistle through the grass
will flex the nerve and batter down these doors.

Hearing your music now within these walls,
watching completion of a thousand years,
sharing the silence of a candle's hour,
moves me again to this late questioning.

Within the chancel burns a light,
and thoughts of incense fill my mind
with dying hyacinths in a room
where I had peace of yet another kind.

Pale shadows weave upon the floor
image and dream and those poor fantasies
that filled my discontented blood.
Now I could lose all those idolatries,

all those ambitions and inflated songs
within one anthem in this ageless night.
Outside, a dog howls through the storm.
Your music stops. The silent pillars wait.

## On Discovering an Old Portrait in a
## Country House

What does it matter that we do not know her name?
To identify her now would spoil the mystery
and place her features well beyond my rhyme.

It is enough to know that once her eyes
looked upon flowers, grass; that once her lips
phrased gentle words, reproached, or laughed.

What does it matter now how old she was?
Should age or rank change virtue in the face
that from dark varnish now looks down at us?

In her calm silence is the history
we care to make. For me she shares this night
like someone loved and secretly possessed,

and I would rather call her simply mine
than see her named and catalogued in print
as someone's daughter or an old man's bride.

## Old Men in the Institute

It would be easy to remember
many things this Spring,
either snow on daffodils
or fires burning under the snow,
yet more than anything
I remember the old men
in the Institute who know
neither the Spring nor burning flower,
whose years turn only on the spit
of each revolving hour.

I remember too their birth –
the prayers their mothers made –
the ache and care and milk
that flowed so hopefully
throughout their days.
Little they thought how hearts would break
and love take lightly to other ways.
Now, in the Institute, alone,
hope is a word they do not know,
unless like Spring and the hidden flower
it burns beneath their snow.

## The Emissary

In the middle of a poem about
joy (and nearly midnight), the door-bell rings.
Stunned by this abuse of my silence
I stare into the shadows on the path
and hear a strange voice break the news
of a friend's death. Whatever cause
I thought might split my house, it was not this.

Grief blurs the details and the stranger's face.
Beyond I see the darkness hung on stars
and feel the trees creep in to hear you speak.
Whatever curse I made you must forgive;
I was for singing when you rang the bell,
but what you tell me changes everything.
Words cannot use the silence that you bring.

## On the Death of a Young Woman who was once a Bus Conductress

That is how I remember her,
ignoring with sad eyes her wartime job,
spending her most generous years
on an old bus, collecting the fares
from shopgirls and schoolboys.

Yet she seldom smiled. Her face
did not wear war's utility beauty.
Deprived of her own lover
she did not seek comfort in the cheap arms
of any soldier that called her.

Travelling home on dark nights
when searchlights taped the throbbing sky
I watched her freeze with fear
as fat hands pawed her thighs for change
or stroked her hair.

Even on days when hedgerows sang
and war was happening somewhere else
she stayed in her quiet world
not falling for our light familiarities.
Pride made her radiant.

Now she is dead and but for this
brief accidental news she might have been
forgotten and grown old. Instead
these words restore for me a girl who once
surpassed Akhnaten's queen.

## Visiting a Country Church

We talked for a long time to the old vicar
hunched in his brown, unsanctimonious coat,
listening as his quiet Yorkshire voice
spent itself freely on our willing ears.

Before he saw us standing in the aisle
we'd watched his simple care for how things looked –
the laundered altar-cloth, the vase of flowers,
the glint of sunlight on cleaned brass –
an old man, putting his house in order for
tomorrow's few.

        Yet this was more than ritual.
Talking about the windows of clear glass
we noticed too his weariness of eyes,
his frail and breaking syllables of hope.

Here was no proud and holy-acting priest
with condescending graces and cool charm,
but a conscientious saint in common dress,
himself worn-out with those twin tasks
of praying for the souls of his indifferent flock
and raising seventeen hundred pounds
to save the steeple for their wedding days.

## The Compulsory Journey

Had your visitors not come –
those early and lost friends from the depressed valleys –
I would not have driven alone into that late
January day between sundown and church-going.

But I am grateful that they came
for I had been without solitude for a long time
and the mystery that lurks in the dark veins
needs to be stripped sometimes of comfort and unchained.

Had the farmlands not been ploughed
I might have seen myself as the first man
walking the solemn earth, myself a guest
praising the unfathomable quantity of space.

But I had with me a ghost
knowing the features of this land, hedges
that made music on their bare thorns, plovers
that scored their black notation on a staveless sky.

And suddenly the journey I had made
because I would not stay and share your past
blessed me with comfort of another kind,
and those dark fields lost both our histories.

*Counterpoint*

High on a ridge of Downs where tracks of history
have worn their tribal patterns on the hills
I feel the past and passing are as one
held out of focus by the afternoon.

    From what damp cave does that old man appear
    to turn his little heap of burning grass?
    What cramped or crippled hands provoke his fire
    or clap with joy around its pagan smoke?
    Rubbed stick or stone or spurting of a match
    can never separate that common act.

Buzzard and falcon now transfix the eye
and poised or dropping down to kill
give rhythm to each necessary death
breaking an ageless cry against the sun.

    What ancient king beneath that ancient mound
    still clasps his rusty fortune and poor crown?
    What royal fear or envy does he bear
    in his thin chains and root-embroidered bones?
    His cattle-grazing grave cannot obscure
    the marble hopes of our own burials.

Below the ridge and twisted spine of chalk
the fields brood on beyond the reach of words.
A stone I throw spins slowly through the air
and shakes a fragile poppy from its stem.

c

What made me stop upon this famous path
to find another age within my own?
What ghost or spirit moves about the grass
to haunt the tribal birthright of my blood?
An old man's fire and a powerless king
cannot explain this day's deep questioning.

## Sitting

My own breathing frightens me.

Sitting through these thin hours of night
by your cold body in candlelight
I dare to hear my own heart miss a beat.

In fear I could cry out,
not wanting yet to share your white
and smiling, newly-taken way.

If dying makes one conscious of this fear
how did you die so calmly?

All's different now
I read in your closed eyes.

Believing this I bend to kiss your face
and feel my sweat freeze needles in my hair.

## A Poem for Two Noble Ladies

Will it come to this
    that the high forest of stone
    will shed its leaves
    and the casual birds
sing in bare branches?

Will the closed silence
    be exposed to the wind
    and the colour of glass
    get blown like dust
from the still chancel?

Then I will write this
    that some may remember –
    that you walked here
    with your prayers and psalms
over aeons of marble,

that here, where a roof
    once sheltered the faithful,
    you sang till the peace
    and the stones shone
in pillars of sunlight,

that here both present
    and past were as one –
    you equal in majesty
    to that sad queen
who, mourning her love,

came alone to this church
    to lie where slow shadows
    work their embroidery
    on living and dead.
    And when in those years

this great forest is dumb
    may they summerly come
    with inquisitive eyes
    to feel both your spirits
and love, rise from the ground.

## Your Country

October is your country
not only for counting tree-rings
but for getting the thumbs stained
purple with blackberries.

You say "I've a thin skin,
that's why the juice penetrates",
yet I know autumn will always
find its way into your roots,

you're made that way. I feel
hedgerows wouldn't be the same
without you reaching up for
hips, acorns and spindleberry.

In fact, I never see autumn
and the bronze haze of sundown
without seeing you as the perfection
of autumn. You are autumn.

That's why I always say
October is your country
and the colours of October
are all the colours I think of . . .

When you no longer come
to show me your thumbs
black with the juice of wild berries
I'll know that I have time left on my hands.

## The Shadow

With you I could have lost
this shadow on the hill,
   the walking ghost
   that at my side
doubles the grief I feel.

I could have locked my house,
turned from that sunless door,
   walked from the town
   and learned to bless
the light and cloudless air.

With you I could have danced
these sorrows off the ground,
   left the cold fens
   and so commenced
the summer of my mind.

But you are shadow, ghost,
a presence that I feel
   stalking the grief
   of winter's frost,
my cold room, and this hill.

## Hillside Burial

Between the dry stone walling of a hill
twelve men are burying a neighbour,
their bare heads barren as boulders,
their throats brittle as dead heather.

There is no priest, ceremony, flowers,
only the shepherds' granite words
committing one of their own kind
to the dark field beyond earth's boundary.

And as they lock his body from the sun
with soil and pebbles of his native land,
each feels the emptiness and loss
left in their fingers by the falling stone.

## Deserted Harbour

We look now at a deserted harbour.
Hives of dry rope are scurfy with salt,
    walls grown over with green nets.

Chains rust, corrode on the quay's rock.
Doors creak in the iron sheds where fish
    were sold. The gulls look senile.

Cottages, defying so long the bailiff-sea,
surrender now to the wind's knock – windows
    and roofs ripped out by an old grudge.

Anchored away from tides one sad-eyed boat
rots on the sand. Even the waiting sky
    looks threadbare and smells old.

No doubt there's little on this northern shore
that we could not, within a wider frame,
    see of our own tired history.

## Death of a Town

The rituals are changing. Old bodies now
are left to disappear without old liturgies.
Dried faces stare like death-masks from sad rooms.
Indifference hides the earthquake of a tear.

Watching those shrivelled hands upon the sill
perched like a desert-bird upon death's tree
I think of how their passing would have moved
our tribal passions forty years ago . . .

    I think especially of that gay child
    we followed through the streets to her small grave,
    of those laments we sang while one dull bell
    silenced the town and muffled the glaring sun.

    We carried flowers all the way
    and saw the pavements thick with crowds.
    Even the uncouth women wept.
    The unemployed joined in our song.

    To be in that procession then, I know,
    was to be conscious of some ageless creed.
    What queen of ancient Egypt or of Greece
    went to their death with so much pageantry?

But age has taken off that noble act.
The preacher's words are drowned by scheduled flights,
and we have barely time to drop a tear
upon the well-kept grass and gravelled steps.

We speed from life to death from death to life
and check our watches by the deafened prayer.
Noise rolls a coat of fur around each stone
before it falls into the speechless earth.

And houses too are falling by the row.
Old rooms with pre-war paper on the walls
release the cries of labour and of birth.
The sky is falling through each open roof.

For some who pass each broken pane of glass,
making their way toward a well-planned State,
some memory is torn, some laughter wrenched,
from each plague-ridden door, each heap of dust.

How long before those taller squares of life
crumble before the fierce, relentless sun?
Old age creeps early to the young child's face.
The desert-bird is waiting, and will come.

## The Flowering Cactus

From your arm
I have been told to pick a rose
when in my ears the sand is lost
and in my shell the sea is locked forever
and made calm,
when on the earth no river flows
and on the hill no bracken grows
to burn itself beneath the sun,
when in Time's bell
season and tempo rush to drown
the words we were not man enough to own.

From your rose
I have been told to sip the wine
when through my side the water moves
and in my blood the mountains melt yet never
find repose,
when stone and star together fall
and earth and sky compose one scroll
no wind shall ever blow undone;
when in my flood
raven and barn-owl fight to have
the hearts we were not brave enough to save.

From your wine
I have been told to taste the rain
when all our valleys have run dry
and in the grape my salt gives foreign flavour
to the vine,
when stillness shall out-pace the stag
and birds and song stay in the egg
unhatched beside the withered thorn,
when from your shape
harvest and blossom grow to crop
the earth we were not wise enough to keep.

From your thorn
I have been told to prick a wound
from which may grow another world
when in my sand the trees may sway forever
newly born,
when plain and pasture gather green
and from your arm new suns are seen
burning our bracken of decay;
when from my hand
music and spring together praise
the flowering cactus and the desert rose.

# A Clutch of Words

To spoil a page,
carve out a dozen lines,
to split a minute
with a clutch of words,
what does it cost?

The patient hawk
drops down into the grass,
flies off with talons
livelier with death,
who, then, has lost?

A thousand light-years
flicker and one looks
to see a hair-spring break,
a falling star,
which matters most?

What are these frail
words written here
but stones or egg-shells
left unhatched
beneath time's claw.